Weird Sea Creatures

ERICH HOYT

FIREFLY BOOKS

A FIREFLY BOOK

Published by Firefly Books Ltd. 2013

First printing

Publisher Cataloging-in-Publication Data (U.S.)
Hoyt, Erich.
    Weird sea creatures / Erich Hoyt.
[64] p. : col. photos. ; cm.
Summary: Illustrated guide to sea life, particularly those organisms of the deep sea, including the carnivorous comb jelly, lantern-carrying deep-sea dragonfish, jewel squid, and dancing jellyfish.
ISBN-13: 978-1-77085-197-9 (bound)
ISBN-13: 978-1-77085-191-7 (pbk.)
1. Marine organisms – Juvenile literature. I. Title.
578.77 dc23   QH91.16.H698 2013

Library and Archives Canada Cataloguing in Publication
Hoyt, Erich, 1950-
    Weird sea creatures / Erich Hoyt.
ISBN 978-1-77085-197-9 (bound).--ISBN 978-1-77085-191-7 (pbk.)
    1. Deep-sea animals--Juvenile literature. 2. Deep-sea animals--Pictorial works--Juvenile literature. I. Title.
QL125.5.H69 2013   j591.77'9   C2012-906747-4

Published in the United States by
Firefly Books (U.S.) Inc.
P.O. Box 1338, Ellicott Station
Buffalo, New York 14205

Published in Canada by
Firefly Books Ltd.
50 Staples Avenue, Unit 1
Richmond Hill, Ontario L4B 0A7

All images courtesy of Nature Picture Library
David Shale: cover, 11, 12, 13, 14, 16, 17, 18, 19, 20, 21, 23, 24, 25, 27, 28, 30, 31, 32-33, 34, 36, 38, 39, 40-41, 43, 45, 51, 53, 54, 55, 56, 57, 58, 62
Solvin Zankl: 9, 10, 35, 37, 44, 46, 47, 48, 49, 50, 59, 60, 61, 63
Jeff Rotman: 15, 26

AUTHOR'S NOTE

Starting with simple curiosity about the deep sea, I have come to know and sympathize with, even to love, nearly all of the creatures in this book. Apologies are due for calling them "weird." Of course, weirdness is in the eye of the beholder. "Normal Deep-Sea Creatures," however, is not much of a book title. I hope your ideas of what is weird will change, too, as you read this book.

I want to thank the photographers David Shale, Solvin Zankl and Jeff Rotman, whose spectacular images made this book possible, along with the many scientific expeditions that enabled them to do their careful, painstaking work. In particular, David Shale and Sandra Storch gave generously of their time to help provide detailed background information for each caption and then kindly corrected my text. David Shale also read and provided valuable insights for the main text. Finally, I wish to thank Michael Worek, Christen Thomas and Nicole North at Firefly, and freelance editor Melissa Churchill.

This book is dedicated to Jasmine Hoyt, Max Hoyt and Morgana Petrison, who may be able to meet these and many other deep-sea creatures face to face some day as the barriers to exploring the deep come down.

— Erich Hoyt, North Berwick, Scotland

Cover and interior design by Jacqueline Hope Raynor
Printed in China

The publisher gratefully acknowledges the financial support for our publishing program by the Government of Canada through the Canada Book Fund as administered by the Department of Canadian Heritage.

INTRODUCTION

In this book you will meet 50 of the oddest animals that live in the sea. Many of them have been discovered by scientists so recently that they have no definite scientific name. Even fewer have a specific common name. Weird creatures ought to get noticed and named. But common names are given to creatures commonly encountered. If an animal lives deep in the sea and manages to avoid capture, then it can carry on indefinitely, keeping its identity secret. If a picture is worth a thousand words, then, for sure, each photo of these 50 weird sea creatures deserves a thousand names.

What makes these creatures odd or weird? More than anything, it is the environment in which they live in the deep ocean — the peculiar conditions to which they've adapted. These include intense pressure far beyond our imagination, and lack of light. In fact, 99% of the sun's light does not permeate below the topmost 330 feet (100 m) of the surface of the sea.

This cast of odd creatures and their deep-sea habitats might seem as far away and improbable as life on Mars. Yet many of them live almost within touching distance in the sense that if you live on the coast or are on a beach vacation or have ever traveled on a cruise ship or ferry, certain deep-sea animals in this book can be found no more than a mile or two away from you. From a ship at sea, for example, grabbing hold of a weight belt or an anchor and taking a deep breath, you could be down among the big-eyed squid and flashing bioluminescent fish in 20 minutes. The problem, of course, even with scuba gear, is that you would not be alive when you finally got near them.

The intense pressure would kill you. It is possible to go very deep in a submarine, but few submarines travel below the upper layers of the ocean. Submarine time for deep-sea-going vessels, even if you can get it, costs the equivalent of King Neptune's ransom.

There have been only two manned voyages to the deepest part of the sea. The deepest spot is the Mariana Trench in the Pacific Ocean, which at 36,000 feet (11,000 m) is 6,500 feet (2,000 m) deeper than Mount Everest is high. The first Mariana Trench voyage took place in the bathyscaphe *Trieste* in 1960, when Don Walsh and Jacques Piccard were lowered to the bottom for a few minutes before concerns about their underwater craft forced them to come back up. In March 2012, *Titanic* director James Cameron climbed into a sub to make the journey, documenting everything he saw for National Geographic.

Two manned voyages to the deepest part of the sea is fewer than the number of manned voyages to the moon (six) and just two more than to Mars (zero), but the fact that they are even on the same scale is astonishing. For us air-breathing, land-loving creatures, the deep sea is impenetrable.

The pressure at 3,280 feet (1 km), where no light penetrates and where some deep-sea creatures live, is 100 times greater than the pressure we feel at the surface. At a depth of 7 miles (11 km), at the bottom, the pressure is 1,100 times that on the surface, or more than 2 tons per square inch. That's the weight of so many miles of water pressing down.

We humans are superbly adapted for life on land, life at sea level. Champion pearl and sponge divers, who use no underwater breathing devices, can reach depths of 100 feet (30 m). Experienced scuba divers can reach 245 feet (75 m) and, with special breathing mixtures, up to 490 feet (150 m). This is nothing compared to the feats of various fish and squid. Marine mammals such as sperm whales and beaked whales can make vertical journeys of 1–2 miles (2–3 km) every few hours.

Adding to the intense pressure, the deep sea is cold and unrelentingly dark. Below the top 330 feet (100 m), which is no more than the skin of the sea, only blue light penetrates. The absolute limit of sunlight penetration is 3,280 feet (1 km) — below that is complete darkness. So how do creatures survive intense, changing pressure in such a cold blackness?

The answer can be found in special adaptations, or traits, that enable a wide variety of animals not only to live at great depth but to move between different depths with different amounts of pressure, light and temperature.

The air pressure within an animal must match that of the outside pressure, or there will be damage to the membranes and blood vessels lining the air spaces and a complete breakdown in normal function. Marine mammals solve the problem by collapsing their lungs and reducing the air space. Deep-sea fish, some of which venture to feed in the upper layers at night, solve the problem with special gas bladders. Those that stay at deeper levels have no swim bladder and their muscles are reduced.

The temperature of the deep, though cold by human standards, is arguably much easier to adapt to because it remains fairly constant with few of the extremes experienced on land and in air. At depths below 3,280 feet (1 km), the temperature is a fairly constant 39°F (4°C). Three-quarters of the ocean has a temperature between 32°F and 43°F (0°C and 6°C). At 13,120 feet (4,000 m), the mean depth of the ocean, the temperature hovers around 1 to 2°C. Exceptions include the hot hydrothermal vents with volcanic activity on the seafloor where unique species have adapted to living in temperatures ranging from 140°F (60°C) to an incredible 867°F (464°C).

The deep-sea currents, though constant, are also more moderate than the wind and wave action at the surface. The deep sea has no hurricanes, cyclones, tornadoes or blizzards. The effects from tsunamis are felt along the shallow coastlines of continental shelves, not in the deeper waters. The deep-sea currents are slow moving. The main water mass in the North Atlantic, the North Atlantic Bottom Water, is created off Greenland and Canada then creeps along the bottom, heading south around the tip of South America at such a slow pace that it can take 1,000 years to reach the North Pacific where it finally returns to the surface waters.

The darkness of the deep has inspired creative solutions. Darkness has forced deep-sea animals to come up with two main strategies to find their food and their mates and to communicate with each other. Some creatures, such as whales and dolphins, use sound. Sound pulses called echolocation allow them to pinpoint the location of food and mates, and other sounds, such as calls and whistles, enable them to communicate with each other over distances of tens, or even hundreds, of miles. But most animals in this book have become masters in the use of light-producing organs called photophores as well as pigment cells called chromatophores. The biochemical emission of light is called bioluminescence.

Photophores are light-producing organs that come in a variety of types, purposes and sizes. Some are simple; others are surrounded by reflectors, lenses, light guides, color filters and special muscles that enable them to adjust the color, intensity and direction of the light they produce. Photophores produce light through a chemical reaction.

Chromatophores are pigment cells that change the color of an animal by expanding or contracting. Sometimes located around photophores, they may shield the reflections of the photophore when it's not active. Squid and octopus are masters in the use of chromatophores for camouflage and communication.

Other deep-sea animals, such as the angler fish with its lure, are able to work with bacteria to produce the light they need in the deep.

The language of light in the deep sea is complex and, depending on one's perspective, either dangerous or beautiful. Pretending we are on board a deep-sea-going submarine with clear portholes, we would gaze out in wonder. Some fish, as they swim by, appear to be carrying lanterns, their bodies only faintly visible in the gloom. The light is at the tip of a stalk sticking up from their forehead or hanging down from their chin. Another smaller fish, flashing fiery

red and blue signals from its sides, in some techno beat pattern, swims toward the lantern, mouth open. A split second later, the smaller fish perhaps senses its mistake as the massive mouth attached to the light on a stalk engulfs it, swallowing it. Instantly, the lights of the prey disappear, every glimmer of light absorbed by the dark gut wall of the predator, the fire extinguished.

Next come the dancing jellyfish and the carnivorous comb jelly (also known as the sea walnut), both of them pulsing in the current, lit up in reds, oranges, yellows and bits of blue. The colors are artificial — refractive colors like the light from a prism or rainbow. They attract prey by looking like an amusement park ride or Vegas sign. They float by as if on parade, the neon messages flashing, then all goes dark. Like all animals they need to communicate in some way with their own kind, but they don't want to signal their location to predators.

After more lantern-carrying fish, we meet the deep-sea dragonfish. And then, looming up from the black, a jewel, or cock-eyed, squid with giant eyes tries to glimpse the light from any of these creatures as it jets by in search of food.

For these and other deep-sea animals, being able to make one's own light has been the key to survival. A few of them have mastered certain special light channels, often red wavelengths, that only animals of their kind can see. Because few animals can see it, the use of red light normally keeps an animal safe below 328 feet (100 m), where no red light penetrates. Those few that can see red clearly have an advantage. The light allows for communication, enables animals to hunt and can help them to avoid predators. Patterns of flashing light can be used for honest communication or for sheer trickery, as with the lantern-carrying fish that give a false impression of their location. Mostly we have no idea to what extent light is used and what message is being transmitted. As with the sounds of whales, the deep-sea world of flashing colored lights is largely a mystery. Humans live their lives on another channel.

Given all the difficulties humans have adapting to deep-sea conditions, how were the state-of-the-art photographs in this book taken?

The possible options might include taking photos through the portholes of submarines, but such portholes are small, fish scatter on the approach of a submarine and powerful lights are needed to see even a few feet into the darkness. Another option might be to lower a camera into the deep, but this would be difficult to operate at the required depth from above the surface, even given knowledge about the day-to-day life and habitat of possible subjects. Combine the logistical problems with the moving fish and squid and the task of getting a clear, well-lit image seems impossible. Even planktonic animals (ones that drift freely) are constantly moving with the currents; fish and squid may dart around. The solution has been to catch and bring the animals to a ship on the surface and then recreate a natural-looking environment in a tank. Nearly all the photos in this book were taken this way.

Collecting in the deep sea is like sampling a pond with a teaspoon. The chances of catching anything are slim. Photographers David Shale, Solvin Zankl and

Jeff Rotman worked with oceanography institutes, museums and the BBC Natural History Unit, taking long cruises to record and to try to understand these little-studied residents of the deep sea. Every day during a cruise, nets and sometimes remote-operated vehicles (ROVs) with cameras and special collecting devices were lowered at various points and to various depths. As soon as the trawl was hauled aboard, the photographers would race to transfer the most unusual animals to fresh seawater aquariums in a chilled laboratory below deck. Sometimes air bubbles or detritus needed to be removed. Most animals were then photographed against a black background using a black velvet screen placed behind the subject. Flash guns on either side of the tank were synchronized to the camera and illuminated the subject against the black background. Once the images were recorded, the photographers did not manipulate them. Shale's stated mission is not only to "catalogue representatives of as many different species as possible, but to present them in the most realistic way."

The most astonishing thing about the deep sea is that these weird sea creatures not only survive the cold, dark, high-pressure conditions, but they flourish. The extent of the diversity of life in the depths is so great as to be simply unknown. Many scientists, however, believe it may rival the most productive and diverse land areas, such as the tropical rainforest.

In 2010 the Census of Marine Life completed its 10-year search for deep-ocean species. This census increased the number of identified marine species by about 1,330, bringing the total number of known marine species to 250,000 with more than 5,000 of these still awaiting formal description. Yet the true number — based on Census of Marine Life findings and a growing body of research into marine life — may one day top one million, or even considerably more, marine species. Each species' successful solution to the problem of how to live and flourish in the deep sea is a result of millions of years of evolution. This means there may be more than one million ways to solve the challenge of how to live in the deep sea and flourish.

As we celebrate weird creatures, keep in mind that weirdness is relative. The ocean comprises more than 90% of the living space on Earth. Even though less than 1% of the ocean has been explored, the ocean, especially the deep ocean, is more typical of our Earth than anywhere on land, such as a forest, a savannah, a city or a shopping mall. These weird creatures are arguably the typical, normal citizens of our planet — much more so than anything found on land.

As you turn the pages and gaze into strange, wild eyes and study these faces with crooked or toothless smiles, you are looking at the fruits of deep-sea evolution. Try to guess what the patterns of lights on their bodies are "saying" and appreciate the artistry of the photographers' work. Take in the wonder, the extraordinary weirdness, of what lives in the seas seemingly close, yet elusive, deep and far away from us.

DEEP-SEA BLACKDEVIL ANGLER FISH

(*Melanocetus murrayi*)

Also known as the deep-sea blackdevil, or Murray's abyssal angler fish, this species usually lives at depths of 3,280 to 8,200 feet (1,000 to 2,500 m), but it has been found at more than 19,685 feet (6,000 m) below the surface. The fleshy "fishing pole" growing from above its mouth is covered in bioluminescent bacteria (a bacteria that produces light) that attracts prey in the darkness. Pictured is the female, which grows up to a size of 4¾ inches (12 cm). The male reaches a length of only ¾ inch (2 cm) and lives as a parasite, attached to the female. It's a permanent arrangement — till death do they part.

WAVY CLIO

(*Clio recurva*)

The wavy clio, also sometimes called the deep-sea butterfly, is a sea snail that floats free in the water. It belongs to the group of pteropods called Opisthobranchia, which means that the gills are situated behind the heart. Wavy clios range in size from ¼ inch (0.5 cm) to ½ inch (1.3 cm).

SEA SNAIL

(Atlanta peroni)

This carnivorous snail lives in the upper 1,640 feet (500 m) of the ocean, where it undertakes daily vertical migrations to prey on zooplankton. It has large, movable, complex eyes and only one lobed foot, which is a flattened fin with a keel that it uses for swimming. The thin coiled shell is so transparent that the interior organs can be seen.

JEWEL SQUID, OR COCK-EYED SQUID (left)

(Histioteuthis bonellii)

Found living at 610 to 1,663 feet (186 to 507 m) depths in waters above the Mid-Atlantic Ridge, which runs south from Iceland, this 3-foot (1 m) squid can often be seen lit up like a Christmas tree. The pattern of photophores, which are the specialized organs that emit a light called bioluminescence, helps to make this squid look like it has a bad case of measles. It also has chromatophores, which are pigment cells that can expand and contract to absorb light to change the color of the body. Other photophores direct light down in the water as camouflage. Its different-size eyes are adapted to the gloomy depths. One huge eye points up, catching light from the surface to search for predators and prey. The small eye searches for predators, prey and mates, checking for the bioluminescent flashes from other animals that swim by.

PIGLET SQUID (above)

(Helicocranchia pfefferi)

Many deep-sea animals migrate daily from deep waters to the surface. With a face like the character in Winnie the Pooh, the small, transparent piglet squid is born in the upper layers of the ocean and moves ever deeper as it develops and ages. This could be called "developmental migration." In this photo, an immature piglet squid displays, just below its short arms, the large funnel that sticks out and will be used to push itself forward. A squid's funnel is like a jet engine. When escaping from a predator, a piglet squid can move itself as fast as 25 body lengths a second.

YETI CRAB (above)

(unnamed; *Kiwa* sp.)

The yeti crab, so called because of its hairy undersides, lives only around deep-sea hydrothermal vents (which are openings in the seafloor from which hot water gushes out). This probable new species was found on the Dragon Hydrothermal Vent Field in the tropical southeast Indian Ocean in November 2011. Yeti crabs are known to collect a type of bacteria called chemosynthetic bacteria on their hairy bottoms, and it is thought that they can harvest these bacteria as a food source.

DEEP-SEA BARRACUDA (right)

(unnamed; *Sphyraena* sp.)

The deep-sea barracuda opens its mouth wide, a three-fang predator smile. It was found at a depth of 1,640 feet (500 m) off Eilat, Israel, in the Red Sea. Barracudas, with their characteristic long bodies, are found in tropical and subtropical waters at various depths.

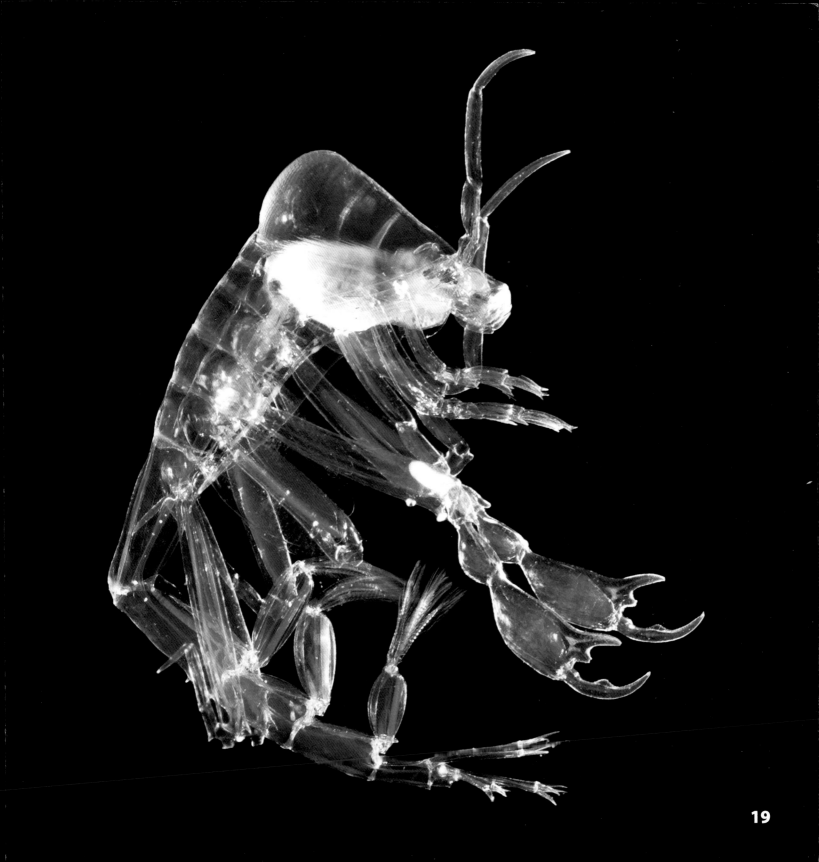

DEEP-SEA SHRIMP

(no common or species name; *Pasiphaea* sp.)

This nameless female deep-sea shrimp — her eyes ever watchful for predators — carries her eggs until they are ready to hatch. The colors of shrimp species vary from transparent near the surface to deep orange or even bright red in the deepest layers of the ocean. In both cases color, or lack of it, provides camouflage. Deep-sea shrimp that migrate up and down in the water column are often half red and half transparent. This female, found in the dark mesopelagic zone between 1,750 and 2,460 feet (530 and 750 m) deep in the North Atlantic, has some color and some transparency.

GLASS SQUID

(Teuthowenia megalops)

Also known as the cranchiid squid, it has large eyes and numerous pigment cells called chromatophores covering its transparent body. It lives in the North Atlantic, where it is usually found below 3,300 feet (1,000 m). The completely transparent juveniles live closer to the surface.

HYDROMEDUSAN JELLYFISH

(Crossota millsae)

This dangerously beautiful jellyfish drifts along the seafloor trailing its tentacles to catch prey — which is whatever might come into contact with it. On contact, its stinging cells, or nematocysts, shoot toxin into the prey. This jellyfish was found on the Mid-Atlantic Ridge, 8,860 feet (2,700 m) below the surface. The reddish colors provide an extraordinary display yet are invisible to its prey. Jellyfish have no brain or central nervous system, and they rely on a loose network of nerve cells to indicate where and when to move in reaction to possible predators or prey.

FEATHER STAR (below)

(unidentified species)

A relative of starfish and sea urchins, this suspected new species of feather star has a typical pose: It uses some of its stiff yet flexible arms to hold on to the ocean floor while it raises its other arms into the current to try to catch and gather passing particles of food. If the feeding is poor, they sometimes let go of the seafloor and swim along by swinging their arms around — a graceful deep-sea ballet. This marine invertebrate was found only in December 2011 and has yet to be formally named.

FANGTOOTH (right)

(*Anoplogaster cornuta*)

Lurking above the Mid-Atlantic Ridge, the up to 7 inches (18 cm) long fangtooth bares its sharp teeth. In fact, the teeth are impossible to disguise; the only question is how wide its mouth can open — up to about 180 degrees. This predator is found between 1,640 and 16,400 feet (500 and 5,000 m) below the surface of the ocean, but the adults reside in the more productive upper layers, from 1,640 to 6,560 feet (500–2,000 m), where they catch fish and squid. The young stay deep — safe from hungry tuna and other predators.

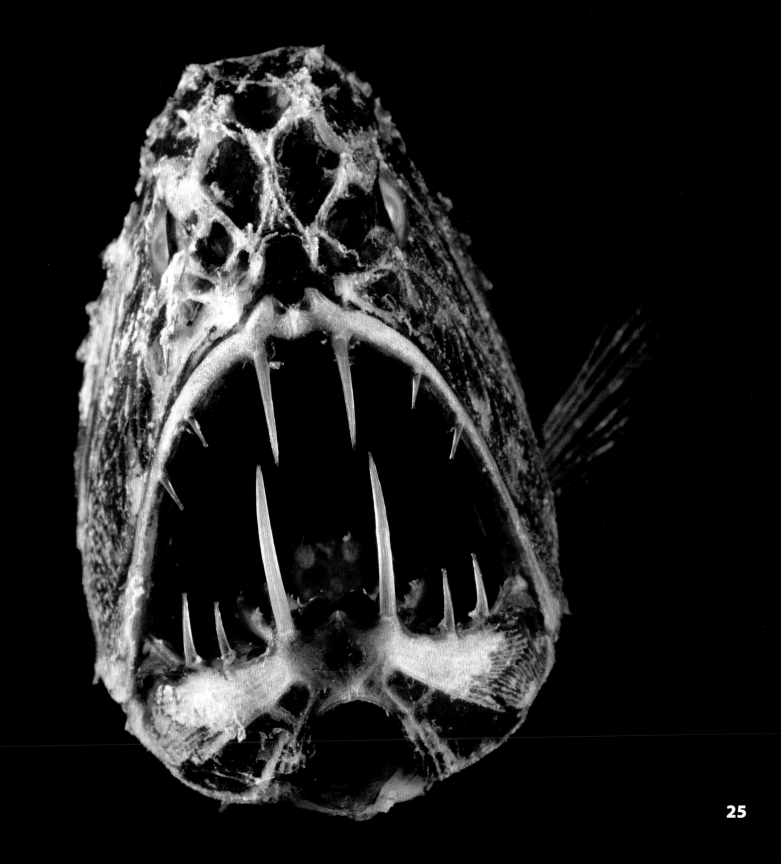

SPINED PYGMY SHARK (below)

(*Squaliolus laticaudus*)

Thought to be the world's smallest shark, measuring only up to 10 inches (25 cm) for females and 9 inches (23 cm) for males, the spined pygmy shark lives at depths of 650 to 6,500 feet (200 to 2,000 m) in tropical waters over the continental slopes. It makes vertical migrations, meaning it swims up and down in the water depending on the time of day, using the luminous photophores (special organs that produce light) on its underside to blend in with the surface and be less visible to predators. Despite its looks, it is not dangerous to humans.

ANTHOMEDUSAN JELLYFISH (right)

(*Pandea rubra*)

Also known as the red paper lantern jellyfish, the name "anthomedusan" means the "flower jellyfish." Whether paper lantern or flower, both names attempt to describe an odd beauty. Living in the deep Gulf of Maine, off northeastern U.S. and Canada, the special structure of this jellyfish, or sea jelly, allows it to fold vertically and compress along what appear to be folds under its umbrella (also called the bell, due to the shape). Jellyfish have no eyes, but some jellyfish have light-sensitive organs called ocelli.

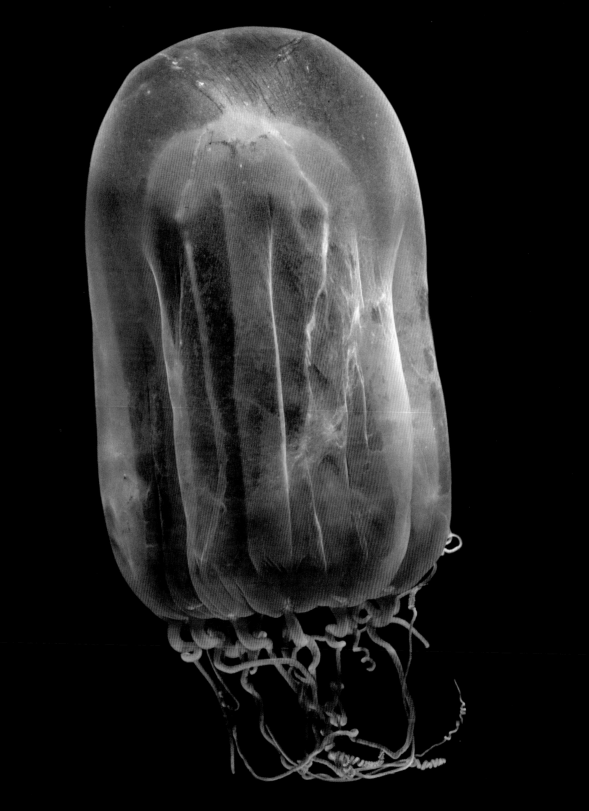

SNIPE EEL (above)

(*Nemichthys scolopaceus*)
When outstretched to its full 16 inches (40 cm) and
hanging vertically in the water, the snipe eel is in its
typical hunting posture. Note the wide-open jaws,
specialized to stay open, which enable it to snare
careless shrimp. When the prey's antennae get tangled
up in the teeth, the snipe eel secures its catch and then
swallows it.

BLACK DRAGONFISH (right)

(*Melanostomias melanops*)
The black dragonfish has no scales and is a slender, up
to 12-inch (30 cm) long deep-sea fish. The fleshy part
growing from its chin lures curious prey close enough
for the dragonfish to seize it in its toothy mouth. Light-
emitting organs along the lower part of its body and
below its eye help it avoid predators through what is
called deceptive illumination. This species can be found
between 1,640 and 2,600 feet (500 and 800 m) deep in
the Atlantic, Indian and Pacific Oceans.

HYPERIID AMPHIPOD (above)

(no common name; *Scypholanceola stephensi*)
This animal is a kind of hyperiid amphipod — part of the order of soft-bodied crustaceans that includes sand hoppers and sand fleas. It lives in saltwater and has been found at depths of up to 29,500 feet (9,000 m). It likes to hitchhike on the outside of the bell of jellyfish. It feeds on small planktonic animals such as copepods. Its deep orange color gives it camouflage in the "red channel" of the deep sea, where few species can see it.

MAUVE STINGER (right)

(*Pelagia noctiluca*)
This medusa, or jellyfish, occurs sometimes in great numbers at the surface. It is found in the warm temperate waters of the world's oceans. It produces light called bioluminescence, which attracts its food. It feeds on smaller creatures called zooplankton, which it catches with its tentacles, using its poisonous stinging cells. In an unprecedented event on November 21, 2007, an invading 10-square-mile (26 km^2) swarm of billions of these jellyfish wiped out a 100,000-fish salmon farm in Northern Ireland, causing over $1 million in damages.

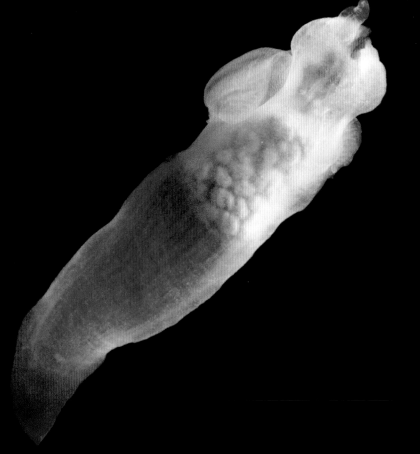

NAKED SEA BUTTERFLY

(*Clione limacina*)

These semi-transparent gastropods, also known as sea angels, swim through cold, deep waters using their two fleshy paddles, which are a modification of the foot of a snail. They might be described as "lovely but lethal" to other small shelled sea snails — their specialized prey.

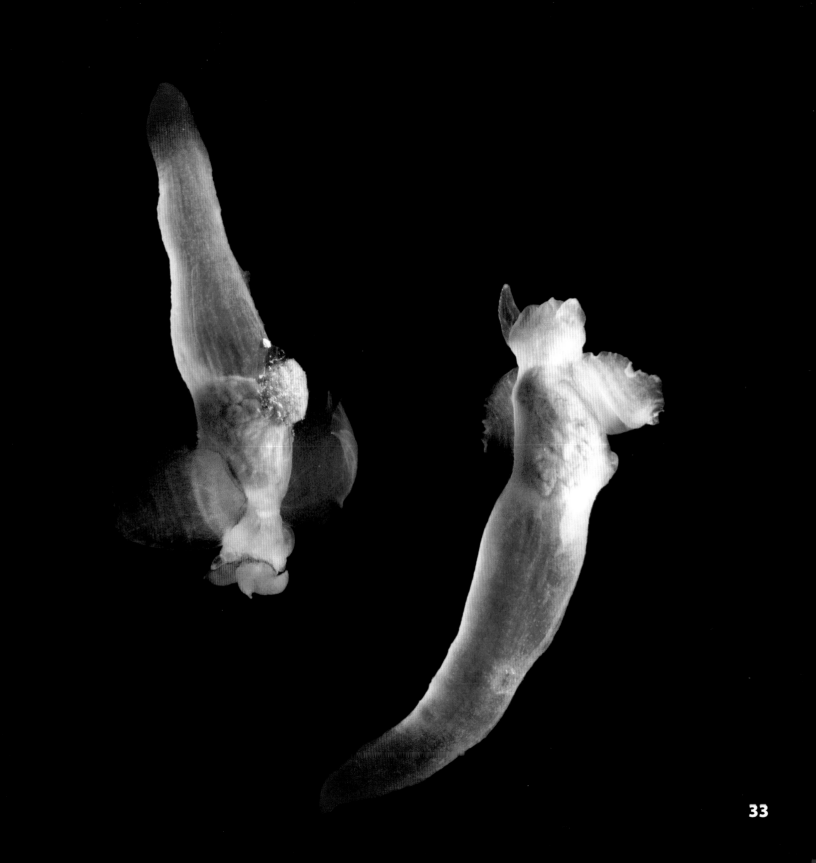

33

SEA CUCUMBER

(no common name; *Peniagone diaphana*)
Most sea cucumbers can only crawl slowly along the
sea bottom. This one not only crawls but is an active
swimmer when it needs to move to new feeding areas.
Its see-through body reveals the simplicity of the sea
cucumber body plan: a simple gut passing through
the center of the body with, at either end, a mouth and
an anus. Sea cucumbers, also known as holothurians,
eat like earthworms. They gulp the soft sediment from
the bottom and sift it through their body for nutrients,
expelling what they don't need. Their key ecological role
is to recycle the seafloor's sediments.

SLOANE'S VIPERFISH

(Chauliodus sloani)

Viperfish belong to the deep-sea fish order of toothy dragonfish found in waters up to 3,280 feet (1,000 m) deep. The pattern of photophores (the light-producing organs) on their bodies emits bioluminescence and gives them a spooky glow. The lights flash in complex patterns, and they may allow viperfish to communicate with each other, or the fish may use them to lure, trick and/or illuminate their prey, or even to confuse potential predators.

BOBTAIL SQUID

(*Rossia* sp.)

The bobtail squid, related to cuttlefish, lives on the bottom of the sea. It has eight arms, each with suckers at the ends, plus two longer tentacles, typical of squid. It uses small fins at the back of its body to swim just above the bottom of the ocean. When chased or cornered by predators it can also resort to jet propulsion, squirting out a cloud of black ink as it pumps water through its body to move itself forward.

PACIFIC HATCHET FISH

(Argyropelecus affinis)
What might a hatchet fish see if it looked at its reflection? Living in the twilight world at depths of 985 to 2,100 feet (300 to 650 m), it cannot see much, but its huge eyes take in as much light as possible, which helps it avoid predators. On its underside, to protect it from being seen from below, the Pacific hatchet fish has organs called photophores that emit blue light, which masks the fish against the faint light of the surface. Hunting under the cover of night to avoid predators, hatchet fish swim to higher depths to feed on plankton.

DEEP-SEA DRAGONFISH (left)

(*Aristostomias* sp.)
As if lit by a Hollywood horror film director, this profile of a deep-sea dragonfish reveals the combination of white and red light that it uses to hunt red-bodied crustaceans in the dark, deep sea. It is also known as the loosejaw fish, referring to its flexible lower jaw, which it can extend forward and appears to be hinged.

DEEP-SEA URCHIN (right)

(unidentified species)
Similar to the sea urchins found in shallow waters, this deep-sea version lives on the seafloor of the Indian Ocean. Moving around on tiny tube feet, it searches for decaying animal parts that drift down from the surface. A sea urchin's mouth is in the middle of the underside of its body. When it finds a piece of food, it uses suckers on the ends of its feet to grab the piece of food, and its teeth scrape away a section so it can jam the tiny pieces into its mouth. Many species of these "porcupines of the seafloor" are armed with poisonous spines.

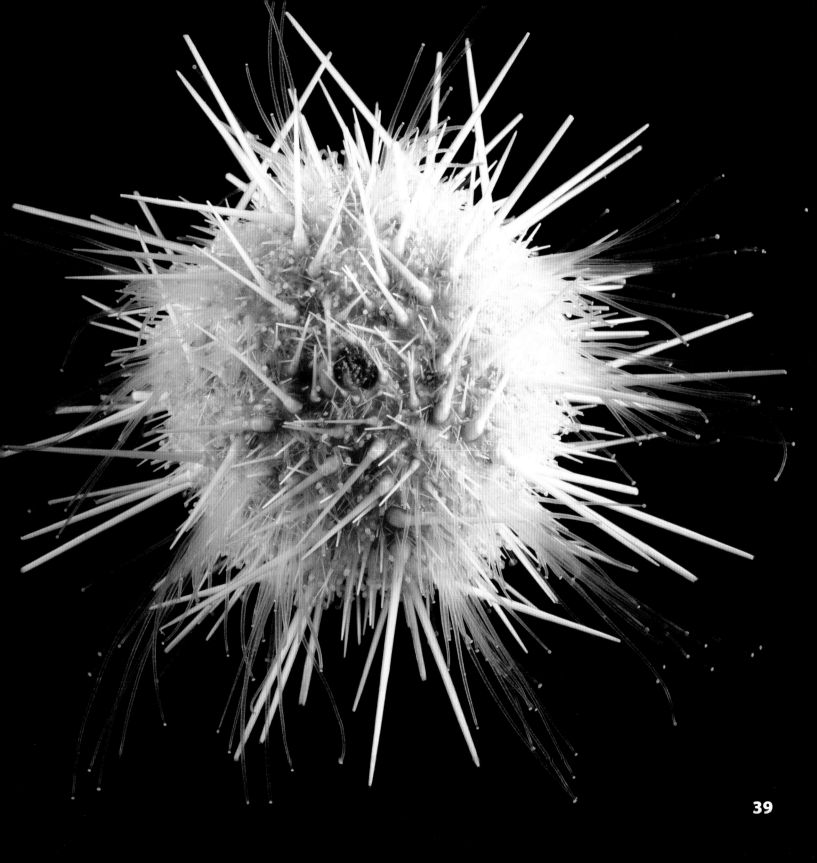

39

ROUND RAY

(Rajella fyllae)

The juvenile round ray is a bottom-living fish found at depths ranging from 560 to 6,725 feet (170 to 2,050 m). It grows up to 22 inches (55 cm) long and lives in the northern North Atlantic and nearby waters. Its back is rough and covered with tiny thorns, especially on its head. It also has prickles on its fins as well as several rows of midline thorns. The arrangement of these thorns changes depending on the sex and age of the ray. The round ray has 30 to 38 rows of teeth in its upper jaw. These teeth are blunt, conical and cusped (meaning they have sections that stick out, like we do on our molar teeth), perfect for eating small crustaceans and mollusks. This individual was found living on the bottom of the cold Barents Sea, off Norway.

found on the Coral Seamount in the tropical southeast Indian Ocean.

43

MESOPELAGIC COPEPOD (above)

(no common name; *Gaussia princeps*)
Compared to the average copepod length of ¹⁄₂₄ to
¹⁄₁₂ inch (1 to 2 mm), this copepod is gigantic, measuring
up to 1 inch (27 mm long). Copepods make up some
60 percent of the sea's marine plankton. Copepods
contribute to the light show in the sea with
bioluminescent effects that include their favorite escape
method: waving their antennae and producing a bright
cloud of light when they flee, confusing predators. Still, it
doesn't always work, as copepods are a main food in the
sea for everything from small fish to giant whales.

DUMBO, THE OCTOPOD (right)

(*Grimpoteuthis discoveryi*)
Called "Dumbo" because the fins make it look like
the Disney cartoon flying elephant, this octopod
has webbed arms that extend almost to the tips and
sensitive tentacles equipped with small cirri (very thin
appendages) along each side of the suckers. A big-eyed
animal, it lives along the bottom of the Mid-Atlantic
Ridge, its orangish coloring making it invisible.

ATLANTIC LONGARM OCTOPUS

(*Octopus defilippi*)

The larval form of the Atlantic longarm octopus shows the early development of the eyes, arms and a few of the pigment cells called chromatophores. When fully grown, this octopus will be 3 feet (1 m) long, 85 to 90 percent of which will be arms. The entire body of the adult will be covered in chromatophores, the pigmented cells enabling it to change its color.

NORTHERN STOPLIGHT LOOSEJAW

(Malacosteus niger)

The northern stoplight loosejaw mainly preys on copepods. This species is in the small club of deep-sea fish able to emit and see red light. The northern stoplight loosejaw shines the red light on its prey, but predators and competitors can't see the predator or the prey. The prey doesn't even notice that it is in the spotlight — until it's too late.

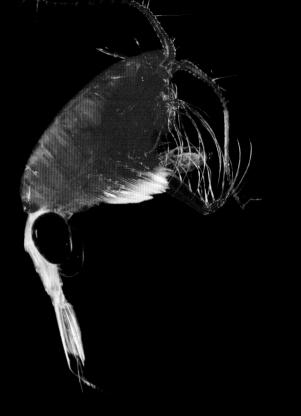

CALANOID COPEPOD (above)

(no common name; *Valdiviella* sp.)
These two female copepods, each about ⅙ inch (5 mm) long, are carrying egg sacs attached to their abdomen. Deep-sea copepods are often red in color, which makes them invisible to most predators in the depths. Although they are mainly planktonic, meaning they float freely on ocean currents, they do have long antennae that they can use to strike backward along their sides, allowing them to advance through the water. With some 14,000 species of copepods, they are the most diverse group of crustaceans.

ORANGEBACK FLYING SQUID (right)

(*Sthenoteuthis pteropus*)
This squid mainly lives in the upper 650 feet (200 m), but it can swim as deep as 5,000 feet (1,500 m). Adults can grow to be more than 6 feet (2 m) long including the tentacles. The name "pteropus" is from the Greek "ptero," meaning wing, named after the pair of muscular fins at the tip of its mantle (its main body), which it uses to move. It is also known to break through the surface of the water, flying through the air momentarily before zooming back down to the depths. The many small photophores under the skin of the mantle, head and arms are grouped together to form a large, oval luminous spot on the back. It lives in the tropical and subtropical North Atlantic Ocean.

AMPHIPOD (no common name; *Epimeria cornigera*)

with LOPHELIA COLD-WATER CORAL (*Lophelia pertusa*)

This crustacean in the order Amphipoda does not have a common name. It lives at depths of more than a thousand feet (several hundred meters), such as above the cold-water reefs off the Norwegian coast, where it was found on this white Lophelia coral. Distributed throughout the northeast Atlantic, this crustacean has a maximum body length of approximately ⅝ inch (16 mm) and feeds on hydroids, which are tiny creatures related to jellyfish.

DEEP-SEA BRITTLE STAR

(unidentified species, class *Ophiuroidea*)
Closely related to starfish and sea urchins, deep-sea brittle stars are members of an ancient group of animals called Echinodermata. They live on the seabed, sometimes thousands of them together, each one raising its five arms to try to capture drifting particles of food — tiny plankton and other nutrients pushed along by deep-sea currents.

SOUTHERN PURPLE ENTEROPNEUST, or ACORN WORM

(Yoda purpurata)

This new species — found in 2010, 12,140 feet (3,700 m) below the ocean's surface above the Mid-Atlantic Ridge — is a member of a group that may be the evolutionary link between vertebrate (with a backbone) and invertebrate (without a backbone) animals. It has the head, tail and basic body plan of a backboned animal but no brain, eyes or known sense organs. It feeds on sediment on the seafloor, leaving behind a distinctive spiral trail.

BENTHIC OCTOPUS

(Benthoctopus johnstoniana)
This deep-sea bottom-dwelling octopus was found living on the Mid-Atlantic Ridge. Most marine species are pale on the underside and dark on top. This gives them camouflage for hunting or avoiding predators. Animals above may not see the dark shape below them, while from below they usually fail to notice the light side, which blends in with the upper layers of the ocean. But the benthic octopus shows reverse counter-shading, being paler on top than on bottom. There are at least 25 different species of benthic octopus living in the sea between 650 and 9,800 feet (200 and 3,000 m) deep.

SEA SPIDER

(*Colossendeis* sp.)

Sea spiders, unrelated to land-based spiders, are common crawlers along the bottom of the deep seafloor. Each of their long, jointed legs ends in a sharp claw. The claws allow them to grab the bottom even in strong currents, and they are their main food-gathering tool. They eat anemones, soft corals and other sedentary or slow-moving animals. They use their proboscis to explore the tissues of their prey and suck them out of their shells.

55

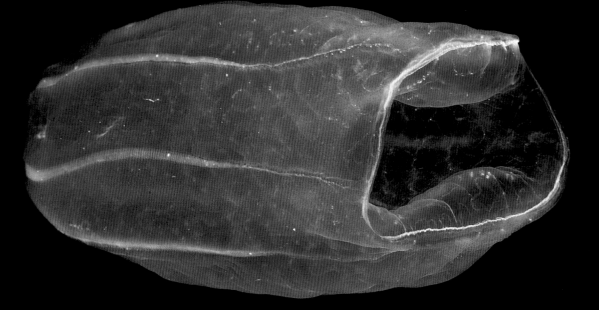

COMB JELLY

(Beroe cucumis)

The always hungry comb jelly (or sea walnut), a ctenophore, might be described as little more than a mouth that swims. Using its rows of comb plates along the sides of its body, the comb jelly swims through the water. Like squid it is also capable of a type of jet propulsion, squirting water from its mouth end to jet around. That mouth is used to prey on other comb jellies, which it swallows whole.

SQUAT LOBSTER

(*Galathea* sp. *or Munida* sp.)
The squat lobster, also known as the galatheid crab, is mostly a bottom-dwelling scavenger. It is found worldwide and at various depths. It congregates in great numbers, scrapping for food around the oasis-like hydrothermal vents. Some squat lobsters living in burrows in deep waters off Scotland have been observed using their extraordinarily long arms and pincers to catch northern krill.

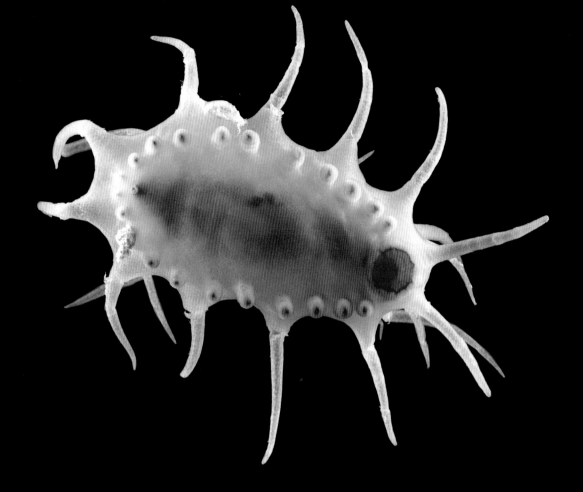

SEA CUCUMBER (above)

(no common name; *Deima validum*)
This sea cucumber was found on the Mid-Atlantic Ridge, some 8,200 feet (2,500 m) down in the North Atlantic. As with other sea cucumbers living in shallow waters, it has a stiff body structure and skin that shows many spicules (which are small, needle-like structures), giving it a rough texture.

DEEP-SEA LARVAL CRAB (right)

(unknown species)
What looks part crab, part lobster and part Sesame Street muppet? Crabs go through various stages of development. The final larval stage, before the crab molts (sheds its shell) and becomes a juvenile crab, is called the megalopa form. It lasts only a week. Megalopa crabs are unable to swim. They are carried by currents, and the lucky ones drift through thick zooplankton patches where they eat as much as they can.

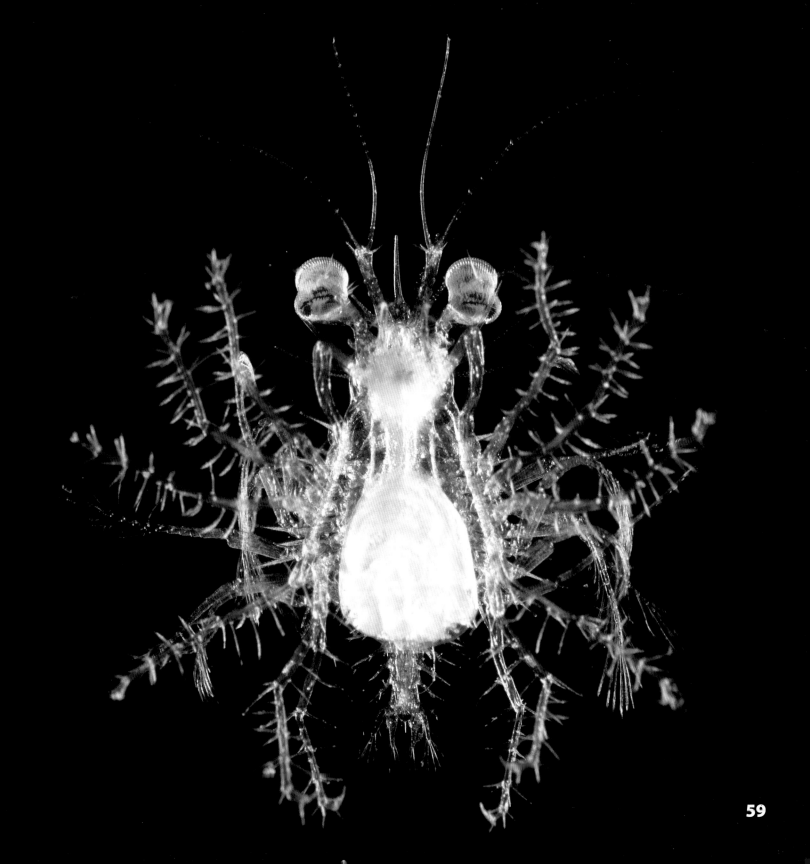

MANTIS SHRIMP LARVA

(Order Stomatopoda; species cannot be identified from larval stage)

The mantis shrimp is a lightning-fast predator that has among the most complex eyes in the animal kingdom. It is able to read even ultraviolet and polarized light. The larvae are frightening and prey on other larval forms, while remaining largely camouflaged in the phytoplankton (due to their transparent bodies). As adults, they will acquire red, green, blue and flashing fluorescent yellow colors and move into excavated burrows or rock crevices, as their eyes, set on stalks, survey the passing food parade. When they see an appealing fish, or shellfish, their powerful limbs uncork, spearing or clubbing the prey, delivering a blow at 33 feet (10 m) per second, equivalent to the force of a 22-caliber bullet. Some species of mantis shrimps are highly promiscuous (meaning they have several mates) and others mate for life, one pairing lasting 20 years.

OIKOPLEURA SEA SQUIRT

(*Oikopleura* sp.)

Oikopleura is a type of sea squirt, or tunicate, called a larvacean, meaning that it stays in the larval form even as an adult. This one, only ¹⁄₂₄ inch (1 mm) long, resembles a tadpole with a translucent rainbow-colored tail. Vertebrates may have evolved from larvacean-like animals. Found in all oceans, sea squirts are tunicates without tunics. Instead, they make secret gelatinous containers that provide them with temporary shelter and allow them to filter water to get their food. Their lives are short: five to ten days. They spend most of their time building and rebuilding these containers, which last perhaps only a couple hours, and feeding as much as possible.

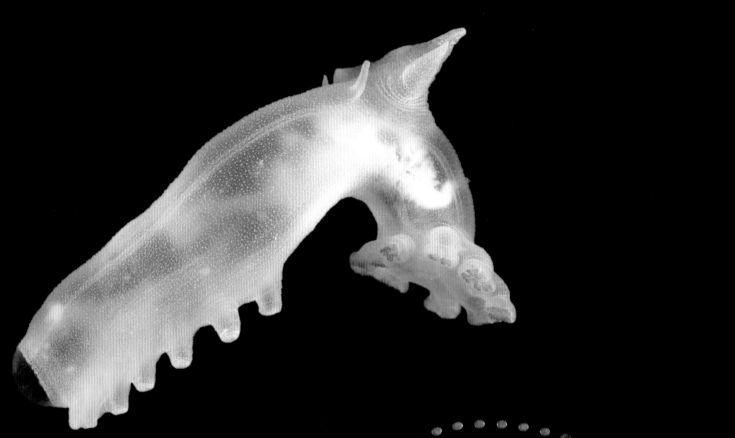

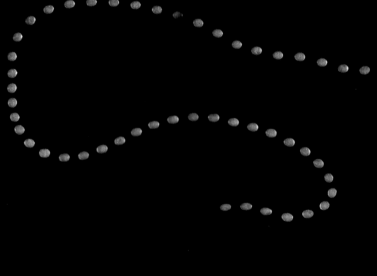

SEA CUCUMBER

(*Amperima* sp.)

If you could walk on the deep seafloor, you would meet
many of these sea cucumbers, or holothurians. This
one was found 8,200 feet (2,500 m) down in the North
Atlantic. Sea cucumbers take their nutrition from the
loose particles that drift down from the surface and
cover the bottom of the sea. This recycling process is
similar to the work done by earthworms to recycle soil.
Sea cucumbers generally move slowly, but some species
can lift off the ocean floor and swim or ride the currents
to move to new feeding areas.

THREE-SPINED CAVOLINE (right)

(*Diacria trispinosa*)

This ⅜-inch (1 cm) long sea snail has a foot that forms into two wing-like structures used for swimming. It feeds on plant plankton in the upper layers of the ocean, and it is known to create mucous nets to harvest the phytoplankton. The plankton sticks to the nets and is then collected and eaten by the three-spined cavoline. Found at a depth of 650 to 1,640 feet (200–500 m), this one was trailing an egg string.

63

INDEX